SWEAR WORD COLORING BOOK

It's Fucking Time for Coloring

Asshole

Damn

Fuck

Jerkoff

Asshat

Bitch

Crap

Holy
Shit

Bastard

Mother
Fucker

Oh Hell

Piss Off

Dick
Head

Cunt

Son
of a
Bitch

Bloody
Hell

Wanker

Slut

Whore

Dumbass

Fat Ass

Fucktard

Prick

Turd

Balls

Dick
Weed

Shit Bag

Twat
Face

Slut
Magnet

Bugger

Shit
House

Fuck
Face

Douche
Bag

Asswipe

Cluster
Fuck

Butt
Munch

Shit
Licker

Goddamn

Fuck
Nugget

Shut
Pouch

www.ingramcontent.com/pod-product-compliance
Lightning Source LLC
Chambersburg PA
CBHW081013170526
45158CB00010B/3024